D1429087

York St John University

3 8025 00627914 8

THE
ROTTWEILER'S
GUIDE
TO
THE
DOG
OWNER

SJ
FOWLER

THE ROTTWEILER'S GUIDE TO THE DOG OWNER

WITHDRAWN

0 9 JUN 2023

EYEWEAR PUBLISHING

YORK ST. JOHN
LIBRARY & INFORMATION
SERVICES

First published in 2014
by Eyewear Publishing Ltd
74 Leith Mansions, Grantully Road
London w9 1lj
United Kingdom

Typeset with graphic design by Edwin Smet
Author photograph Alexander Kell
Printed in England by TJ International Ltd, Padstow, Cornwall

All rights reserved
© 2014 SJ Fowler

ALL ERRATA IS INTENTIONAL,
AND THIS WORK HAS BEEN
THOROUGHLY PROOFED
SJF

The right of SJ Fowler to be identified as author of
this work has been asserted in accordance with section 77
of the Copyright, Designs and Patents Act 1988
ISBN 978-1-908998-20-0

SJ Fowler is a poet,
artist, martial artist and vanguardist.
He has published five previous collections
of poetry, been commissioned for original works of poetry,
sonic art, visual art, installation
and performance by the Tate,
the London Sinfonietta and Mercy.
He is the poetry editor
of *3am magazine*
and curator of the Maintenant series
and the Enemies project.

TABLE OF CONTENTS

Atacama

.

like with women
the desire for multitude
leads to a certain solitude

*

does this work support me in what I truly wish to do?
or does it paralyse me, promising the achievement of a spectre
while maintaining conditions of that paralysis

*

chacabuco foam, they took to take her teeth
deprived of her enemy
she shucks dust

*

if it's still human
& fine weather, in the admin. of stars
on the clarity that isn't the bottomless
of rather a dead mother – by tractor
those contests of dead chests
proudly thrust out forward

*

and the gasps of love, after all, had got him
ready. john berryman

*

the made comes like a swelling vision
an eye cracked beneath, good stoppage
the past are taking over
from the time it takes for my eye to see
the light that it has been agreed
will be let go

*

chilean watches are the best movement
like a rat that was scorched by flame
and filled, rowed up in old slaveminer's houses
tranquill waterless mountains
many a man here lies, holding holy shit
only the sin that laid them low
knows how they forgot life

*

the tractor digger furrows
the sand & in so did
get to doing
the devastation of the skeleton's integrity
bits as in teeth chics
fingertips and bone chips
spilled out the side thresher

★

an unfortunate
accident for the searching
mothers

Epithalamia

{for livia dragomir}

THE ROMAN WIFE

a horrible love that ends a massacre
burn ours as the twin to a jungled war
imply the notion of a kind end
smothering a poem about the high end
the tower of escape into hours
get it for all it means before it was
that we won't be lonely again until one of us dies

PORCA

> It follows me like someone that hates me
> *Jack Spicer*

when I saw you in the morning
that was when I realised (I had explained) we had slept
& today was the day   Granada -
it doesn't matter how you die
heart attack, shot in the back
of the head
the dead wear the same wings
as long as they have shoulders

helps got the shudderless dead

BEAUTY I'D FURROW

say you'd
        fox
& reply mush
            room
covered in deer's shit
life giving
political
fruit
hard MIND clean
of thick skin
thin vein
for when I sleep

you tangle my face
in cob   no wonder
the Pope to flies is awe
          inspiratio

MEMLING

there have been depictions
of skeletal horses still animated
ready to drag a carriage
through the night
a simple calculation – our
marriage is a kind of dead horse &
I have spent my life preparing
the nest

CLEFAIRY

> These worlds make the friendliness of human
> to human seem close as cup to lip
> *Jack Spicer*

she wouldn't be
the cloud
a minor silver out of Târgoviște
& of the others
not married

her
softly killing soon
falling feet;
shotgun blast

BECAUSE HE LIKED TO BE AT HOME

don't bid hidden, equator
not when you've made us all so
hot for then where would be the upside?
the not-rain? I'm not a-fussed
Ambassador for the paraolympics
my parents profession doesn't really either

UNICORN BABY SHOWER

unison singing future family folkbank
a herd of buffalo's trying to fly is AIDS apparent heir
we'd never go to marry new york when it was enough for
mexico
heat & even the women said she looked beautiful dressed
as curbs of terror
are all the more risk of horror now
DON'T RUIN it

PENDULUS RABBIT

forewell to thye dungeon, I do them
the musk hunt in the mountains
the bears of Romania are now I am
tie your bin bags tight for the smelt
holding hands, first her right through my left
then both hands, opposites
easier to eat the grass
for our days repeat after me
easy work for the straw
scarecrow again burning

LIMP

the actual words
a little belly
singing a song of fingers fed;
today is a day of finger chopping
though it is not those 9 who have slept
no lips - I said the words right
the leg, the fassbender   has gone dead
& close the window
some do not want to hear the crying
others not laughing

THE PHOTOGRAPHER

for A.Kell

the photographer friend, which
makes it complicated, has a golden axe
which makes himself see geometry
& not people
can we move the register into light
for the photograph to work?

THE LIME CAT

surgery
a bone / a bare mare / question the centre
a marrow like an aubergine
the not bread
an expensive breath
the choice is a very real choice
& was never no threat to no man or woman
we have plenty of spare days
plenty of holidays
but we know in which work closes off at
holding a windpipe between finger & thumb
like the switching off of a lightswitch
in the meantime, I'm only on my knees
for the garden
sweet potato

URSINITUS

> Trees in their youth look younger
> Than almost anything
> *Jack Spicer*

using a bear
as a child's gravestone
the green balloon
just out of reach
seems agonising
& reiterant
of the symbolic
slipping through
of the dead baby
I hope that doesn't happen to us

PHAROAH MONCH

black banana
a little song of two
the chair in the crypt
& those who will never be sitting on it
those who flower
golden, & Russian
for the two who fold the chair
that was made of wood, & flowers
the diagnosis is a cup
in the hand held
but facing the wall

& not the street
the two, like breasts, are two
great & free, & outdoors

A BURNED GROUND

> Everyone is impressed with courage
> *Jack Spicer*

a burial ground
at 2.30 in the afternoon
... could not remember
the time set to meet
I see a tower with a clock & remembers

NATIVE

> I carry the No you gave me
> Clenched in my palm
> Like something made of wax
> An almost-white lemon
> *Jack Spicer*

love
if half days were the half-day
that would be common
in Marylebone
beasted by the bull

marsh-thieves every
one
who'd have thought I'd owe
a reward for the past
decision to not
desecrate the funeral gold mine

USEFUL O WOULD HAD SPRUNG,

> Isn't she ever coming?
> *Jack Spicer*

useful ((O)) webbings
are better
than all
the others:
unknown
where something is smaller
through the door
than it looked in the room
a cork candle, & cakes
celebration means
weddung in city-sprung

LOVE EATS The EYES

love eats the eyes
not making contact
during
shrinking
   chinese
      moon
it couldn't have been better
but it could've been worse
the possible
ghosts on the house sitter's troubled sleeping
the dreams are no more
in Paris
than in London
so that's another clean – unclean

BONECHIPS

> It is not unfair to say that a city is a collection
> of humans
> *Jack Spicer*

we saw post in Paris they'd had poems impressed
(embossed) & I'd wanted to make some for England
black boned chips they're made of
& the loud crowing in the mountain
turned against each other
won over by compromise
settling the balkans aright

fools to build the bark
it'll sink as long as no one fights me we'll be fine
yep better left in Paris passing

THE GRAIL

> Youth
> Is no excuse for such things
> Responsibilities
> Weigh like strawberries
> On a shortcake
> *Jack Spicer*

I have wife enough
a riddle
am I
a-king now?
to who had the idea: to who helped
in whom I love worlds ... so far ... as much:
as one word
to toe those enough to have
don't spoil
me
I'm not that as the thing
as when finished
until I have to wait again
for you to arrive

Wormwood scrubs

in awe of the life's writing > Anselm Hollo
(april 12th, 1934 – january 29th, 2013)

o my best friend
bones
if i should die

≠

all those emails unanswered
might be a tiny ear
in the palm

≠

on wormwood
that's why
holding you so lovely

≠

its
almost always
a love poem here

≠

command is given
& we're clan
free above the wall

≠

before where the lion teases an army
its more silky
as it lifts its tail to the whores!

≠

to have to two wives
two sisters / two mothers
& 3 dragons

≠

how did you get those
bruises?
    sport

≠

singing to me about eye colour
performance poets
lublin isnt dublin

≠

& the feelings in the heart
of feelings
but 12 year old nearly dead through self starvation

≠

refusing potassium pills
the only way to stop the father
is to kill him

≠

there is nothing pathetic
about her
she doesnt panic

≠

what colour need a spoon be
when bored into thick
in order to stir shit as profession

≠

the city a snake
turns out a shark
doom, the house rises up into a man

≠

o my david
butler & friend & best man
you're nothing on my wife

≠

were it not for an old bear
reading
we would free miniature licence

≠

to love
just days from that old letch
informing us how love we are

≠

& will be
apart from everybody
because ain't we not like them

≠

a crocodile bird
a line of matamatas
            surviving videos, like wolves

≠

borobudur from the outset
there are two discretions
the first on objection

≠

lie I
on wormwood scrubs
profusely sweating, kettlebells

≠

o creatine Monohydrate
mate
snitches get stitches

≠

cock tree lays iron egg
nearing thirty
we should've listened

≠

no things fall apart
a sign in those horse bones
ash into yuan, the first memory

≠

today backwards riding an electric horse
galloping into the lid
atop a void

≠

you will leave some trace (un)fortunately
now something new
instead

≠

so much
noise
at home (love; too brief)

≠

finally knowing the near dead
clean, just for a moment
you're a slag

≠

the clumsy odd
a family friend for fourteen years
now plant stalks your daughter

≠

the baby won't pollute
don't turn to the micro wave
fire if just fine

≠

mountain fist, ocean mouth? avalanche
tidal wave
where will the casio be hidden?

≠

pishhead tradition winding up
in intervention / or death
timely sobering

≠

on the banks of the yellow & black
don't live in leeds
beat quieter

≠

o no a peck with an acorn!
turns out a small knife cuts demons
when accurately thrust

≠

a river in the marble
harvest shrapnel
four ways / one hat

≠

I was olivia
nicolescu
& I make suicide

the Rasenna

The fascist is young-
Why does he carry a teapot
Among the graves?
Araki Yasuasuda

I.

battered squid in blackened
moonlight
is bound to be bitter
&there is bound
to be a schoolgirl
in there somewhere

II.

a painting, a poem
a sculptures
a severed head
all are a disappointment
in the grounds of the hot castle

III.

a beautiful young
wife weeping
& his six days out
a Polish / Brazilian / Lithuanian
                - French
the lithe coat, the clutch flowers
I understood, but why? I asked
these are, he said, arms held out
my only penis, & I must be done with it
before we head
                off

IV.

a love litter
willing
to you
who risks
widow
to pain
sorry
you're so hard even there
& may one day not be
 (what a
waste – I had waited all week
to say something nice
& instead
again
I am just left
pointing out the faults
of others.)

V.

tugging her pasta alternatives
from the black ram
I realise we are loving
upon a rug
& shriek
my manhood has left me
& she calls me a 'girl'
just as I feared
the stonecold climate of growing up in Newquay

VI.

I am to forget my house is in the trees
turning over pines to look for girls
i want to fuck but cannot fuck
my house is in their hair
because
that is as close as I can get
as they enter, the others
treat them as though
they have returned from the dead
geisha to a lord
saltwife to a cheat
it is a new spring
better left to those *others*

VII.

remember when you were young
to someone singing
remember
when you
were young
well
now your children walk on their hands with their legs crossed
they walk in the park
& their lap beneath their groin
& in their teeth is an X-ray
& a scar across their belly that looks like the beak
of a stork
we have children now
no more time for
pink floyd

VIII.

watching
that private bit of american psycho with huey lewis and the axe
i realised the suffering was in advance
she was paid, and forced, to purse her lips
and suck
the vegetable impression of a girl
friend
its awful to be occupied by a disease
that makes you different
than before
and other people
like shaking uncontrollably

IX.

poppy capsule full of powder
how can you harm my body
so much larger than the granules?
child with a screwdriver
hardly a threat
the robin paces on the doormat
the heat kills wind
the question is a surgery to friendship
a man wants a man
a cat wishes for death
falling often lands
our dad died at christmas
it is mostly unfortunate
but entirely it is nothing really
to wander about

calling the doctor makes
me feel better

the way man uses music
to kill in one day
what he bred in one life

*

the way man uses black people
the way to use a simple goblet
as a hitting weapon
so i wish to use
the excellent poetry of other people
(note the stress)
that my two dozen readers haven't read
to fashion my own Season
between water and spring
covered in scales

*

a man just stepped on my toes
I'm too good to be (un)known

★

the sound of the human body
falling without resistance from five feet
is subtle

★

temporary workers live in every
slice of year round
the pint glass our union bleeds into
who makes it harder on themselves

★

honestly, being shoved by a shavepate
is an honour, and have you I've
noticed the disproportionate amount
of enormous men who are the police?

★

lucky for us they learn confucianism
and our poets in university
really understand the nature
of poverty and violence first hand

Scent

KRAMPUS

if you grow just a little bit taller
then I promise, I will learn to love you
or is that the other way around
what is the scent of that, mapping out the future?
of ballet in a nightclub
of cleansing for a compliment
the fragrance of an Alp

SOAP ROMAN

I'm smart enough to make my
own soap
out of my own fat

BOMB FOG

the fog
has its own
scent
we trick to
capture

CAT CANCER

road measures life in distance
the further you travel < the longer you live
trained of being a perfumier
rather than a doctor?
like a veterinary failure, worrying over
cat cancer
rather than blood tests
& then I saw the afterbirth
edible

FLUB

flab of ambergris
between lid & eye
feel the hartpoon
penetrate whale

POMMEL HORSE

ascent for tourists:
horse skin, cooking meat
& faint animal shit
to remark upon
not being welcome
& not normally very clever & loud

COFFIN PINE

the scope of human stupidity ends not at the bounds of smell
as things could be life giving for ease & longevity of life
but are not, & will not be
cruel portion, never enough time to cultivate
        the sense
what will perfume matter?

SKIPS

there are men in blue overalls & young girls with red scarves
who smell nice
who I smell after they have walked past me
on my left, a freckle faced woman sells plaster casts of Venus
and slices of yellow cake
the fruit stall on the right must have caught fire
charred apples and oranges steam in a puddle of water

an old woman in an army coat swears at a child
six beautiful pheasants hang limply from the side of a bicycle rack
I'm not buying anyone's perfume today
I'm off to school
my fingers. still smelling

BATH DEATH

1st bath: red water, a sheer curtain cliff, a frog, the door open
2nd bath: a round ball bull, both for two
3rd bath: a cavern of blue water, a liliger's pond, slow drickle, lofty home
4th bath: scared, a natural bridge, some terrible stats on that, so cut that out
5th bath: a water theatre – friends of Toronto, better it helps muscle than hurts it

GORILLA ATTACK RECOVERY PROGRAMME

gorilla attack recovery program massage bar
i can't help you enough to deal with this attention
the silverback is called snowflake
in my chair, I am asked "why you bored, you just sit in chair all day"
to which I say "be off grommet, the beach is for locals"

FUN SOUP

overconfident with a manta ray
we where the fish were
danced
seeing fish in every lap

AZTEC BLUNDER

searching your lost love for stolen supermarket goods
working to clock
set lunch hours signalled by a siren
this is the potion of the people
ghost towns
an overweight elderly hairdresser overheard
saying "...exicans have been decapitating
peeple for thousands of years
it doesn't mean there,
what it means here."

RICH POISON

the man selling rat poison shows a pile of dead rodents to prove his
efficiency
the tooth puller displays a heap of teeth to prove his skills in dentistry
his gaze is unnerving
I suspect there are dog teeth and pig teeth mixed in his pile
how goes the man who is selling perfume?
an upturned wrist as a theme to the jolts
like an electric throne & he's got a Malaysian wife
yea, don't we all mate

ABATTOIR OF CHILDREN

abattoir of men, is it implicit
that the worst is going on while you scent?
the sky will be serrated in three pieces
blood will always spill like it were bottled
and as magicians do, I will always
try to help everyone in the room until they die

MOTH WORSHIP

is it blasphemy to say priests have sex with animals?
aubrey beardsley died so young in an age of giants
tangled in the bubble fence
I could say worse but my love won't let me
why only in the west do we need our sex scentless?
said Spaniard, forgetting moors.

A RUN ON

washed for birthday wolves
people have run out
of ideas
I am hard to buy for

they let me have his books

{for james harvey}

from the balcony of gordon sq.
i spy holly, rocio, tom and jose
                    with octavio
they are like monsters underground
eating handfuls of coal
only to discover blue diamonds

*

we are like patron queens
inviting the contented to their death
politely, & with courtesy
& we are a community
this is what James' death has taught me

...a few days later

he was called schmidt
and though he spent too much on books
his psychoanalysis was material

*

too much criticism for certain speaking events
but then we all realised in the newspapers
how much they cost
the seagull returns, travelling
she has grown needy
and through worry
is so negative to be unbearable

too much aspirin and it drowns

Wildermenn

Wilder, Telfs, Austria

it must be admitted that a fit of rage
or a sulk has its secret attractions
were that not so, most people would long
since acquired a little wisdom

Wilder, Telfs, Austria

exhaustion pay is bank double
the forest burns bush green hair
hides a thing at the information
desk

Perchten, Werfen, Austria

if i could quell this search for justice
says the Wilderbaren, I'd not have had
sex with all those there girls bodies (in an alley)

Perchten, Werfen, Austria

hunting today
made her laugh using the word
photosynthesis

Krampus, Bad Mitterndorf, Austria

I will not be moved by you
    Chamber of horrors

Krampus, Bad Mitterndorf, Austria

to the age its art to art its
scorn for the Oberwildling

Chriapa, Ruzomberok, Slovakia

I know huntsman
who just have to hunt
            untilitgetstothegutting

Medved, Ruzomberok, Slovakia

the famous chicken spends a day
before   the beast finds her
in the magic circle
I even censored it in my head + one day I
will censor it as it happens

Smrt, Trebic, Czech Republic

superhuman power
Eros is a mighty daemon as the wise diotima said
endure! as long as man has an animal body
& it is not just about the gong

Laufr, Trebic, Czech Republic

why is it that we are especially
interested in psychology now? the answer
is that everyone is in desperate need of it

Certi, Trebic, Czech Republic

devaluation of the real woman
need to return to non-sickened worship
of female body – bush, tongue, hips, line of arse
its taste – not just in the night

Certi, Nedasov, Czech Republic

heavenly people as the reason to dress lost
in toothpummice
pune honey pool

Macinula, Cisiec, Poland

can I not have the marriage moment pure?
& that unwashed on the 4th tower

Dziady Smigustne, Dobra, Poland

AIM scared. it never stops when imagining
the invention of killing a human body
could you look into it?
  scums overfrost

Strohbar, Ewattingen, Germany

barber
yawns
red egg nimble

Reisigbar, Empfingen, Germany

fat of the bone
sugar of the brain
ear of the appendix

Erbsenbar, Empfingen, Germany

the laugh of the bear
releases prisoners

Strohmann, Empfingen, Germany

peasants twist in fear
for their arm lust
in coming

Strohmann, Leipferdingen, Germany

conquest animal sets sail on a Strawboot
raw honour of the boar
brigade
a social club / trade union

Pelzmartle, Bad Herrenalb, Germany

pay for slaves with smiles / or spears
widow to a
goat leans and can still Climb

Tschaggatta, Lotschental, Switzerland

my auntie is paris 'Lord a bones'
bonjour tristesse translation
meat for arms / bones for suit

Peluche, Evolene, Switzerland

there's this stupid frat boy gnome
where they would tie
  4dozers with ducks
    tape   Weeblie

Wortwedding

TREPIDATION

don't change the plans at the last minute so that each person who makes up the room
that is this room who was come to be defined by that which they came here to watch
may quickly find that I don't think as much as I should about their being in love
with their work colleague or neighbour for I am not so timid as not to say
anything about that and change that which particularly concerns me within
the compass of this lesson that is here to be allowed in Berlin
where I am to speak from the centre of a language while my dance partner will
offer me a mattress of paper which floats about our nervous chats
so that I may speak clearly in an Nglish that you all understand
& of course you have come to know a journey to be here through the snow
and didn't imagine you would face a motion that might be dance and is not the practise
of tactile familiarity to throw or trip another human body to the floor
to end up beneath or to deflect the swing of a knife which you have no chance of deflecting
and then an address of that journey you undertook in gratitude
pleased to be indifferent to how we have been sought out
when of course   but not considered   there are things at play which you cannot know
in my experience over the last five days since I have been here in Berlin
knowing this performance would come & no doubt you have read your textbooks
from the guild of a dance company that lives in a prison is just a moments' walk away
and we have all here visited that website which offers opinions
on whether I personally should invest in property in Neukolln or Wedding
yeayou laugh   as if it were possible in this city   that someone who is addressing
your journey as though it were the subject for poetry could have enough money
to also own property even in a place as cheap as one that has no readily available work
for the iron women on rudy dutschke   that are pretending to wear the full hijab
and walk five steps behind me but listen carefully and you can hear their tools
being readied by the striking of a clock in the night's deserted hours around here
where there are no nightclubs no bars no ready alcohol and from my high window
as if in a poor painting of a singing voice being strangled in the past I have the cold
blown upon my fingers and realise in these words like a child
that it's a shame for my first lesson to point out that good things happen for bad reasons

ACCOMMODATION

good morning alessandra and her friends, and monika and Nicola and livia
please feel free to sit down upon the floor and the wallpapers which has been stripped
away to not be replaced as though there might have been discovered
the remnants of a child who had to be hidden and was not forgotten
but could not be reached for who is the woman saying come here come here
which is almost the same in german as it is in English and who has yet
to notice berlin is the new Malaga in that its primary import besides pineapple
is a curtained generation of the Nglish   we find away like reptilians to speak
to a young man with talent and the rarer gift of assurance and climbing boots
I have been thinking about the progress of these lessons of how they might
be defined by themselves as we wait for them to grow into something aside
from themselves that are not defined by a video projection of silent minutes
over sixteen days which is a flat country of a certain time in the morning
where I was normally found becoming a musician of a certain character
practising the song mcduff again again down the manhole let the sky fall
down into a heap of bad drawing artists and dancing girls who stack their impressions
like horrifically bullied seasonal workers in Hessland who make me wonder
how easily I would impress them with my newfound attractiveness
and how many I could get to the moment of investment because money
IS such a serious business in any language at the moment of the moment
that needs to be translated into a hammer shaped sickle crisis of the moment
now we must try to lift ourselves higher says the voice aware of the terrible
shape of noise that is outside that very window behind us now
where at any moment we might be mocked by groups of children
who know only one way they might reach us by breaking our fragile feelings
and I for one propose we play them my aforementioned song to hurt them
emotionally right back and if that doesn't work then we search them with our
superior numbers and run. so ends the second lesson.

INTIMIDATION

now we must try higher anxious   to define this group smuggling
but at least we aren't alone in wanting to learn music here and so we can be a group
anxious to love each other or am I assuming too much because that is what I assume
even though honestly I am not comfortable with that idea at all
and I'd much rather be alone right now let alone in our love filled future
remember the silence broken by my music is curious about its blood family
but not so interested in those that might be called the adoption agency
and its client elements which you all shall learn to represent
when the radiation from Fukushima arrives and every man's sperm dies
and then we'll see if the divorce settlements remain at fifty percent
but for now standing in the correct position with the wood beneath our feet
at a perfect right line with our feet the foundations arose inside of us a balance
which will produce children of clear unchained starts and finishes in living
that will match us and define us by being there at all able to speak words
back to us like these words but hopefully more inventive and poetical
and clever and political as though these children of ours can use their brains
as ocarinas, or flutes, into which they speak and make another hold delight their elders
a fat chance, they will all be late and traverse study taken lightly
until we don't care anymore, almost the way you feel about what I am currently
saying because I have tried your patience by not making eye contact
and reading from the paper sheet while my collaborator tries to make you
listen I, like your children, could care less though don't mistake this paper shield
as a shield for my protection, but for yours, for if I were to look up now and again
to emphasise a word it would be you who would be harmed
like the hand in the cornerplace fire which warmed people in a time
when international torture journals were bursting with Content
this lesson shall not be prolonged like a ladder that is just too short to reach
those trapped in the upper windows of a burning apartment block
of which in your city there are so many to choose from I almost don't know
where to begin with my petrol and my lighter which reads welcome to berlin
and now fuck off home foreigner and I have to laugh you used to do this
kind of exclusion so well but now it all seems a watered drink
good stances you are still standing strong feeling the heavy pregnancy
emerging from the floor to unswell your head and keep your pitch from wandering
to your other interests aside from the art that is one more piece of wood
burning in the welding mask that must always remain light to wear if we are to learn

VARIATION

be varied in your words as varied as the noises in your mind otherwise it's just noises
(but that isn't interesting asks the one in the front row who will learn)
like choke choke choked laugh laugh chalk chalk chalked
the mind is not a violin to be tuned it is a thing that can await the inevitable
return of its own sound and process that   and give that a name
my flat land pays me to dance in another room   not this room where the adults are
sipping our coffee and talking reasonably and profitably about our projects
which kill the time being killed by the children in the next room
clapping their hands, clicking their thumbs and stamping
as their waists swing in one repetitive motion that is attached to their arses
but I am only bitter because I cannot make a song   only discuss it awkwardly
and I'll have to return the money and live off the contentment of knowing
I made you a little better by being worse than you think you can do
and allow you time to think about how red the stove is and how you would be handing
me the matches and seeing your handiwork glowing better
were it not for the words and the noises and the recording feedback and the videos
all distracting you for at heart you wish you were just in a church hall hearing
a

  sermon written just for you and being heard only by you that comforts you
so you might be famous to have said only you heard the great meister
as he confided his poetry in you that spoke of the impossibility of knowing
what can't be known especially if there's four things going on at once
muddling the senses, and the fire too today thinking of you as the great creator
as if we were all early this morning arguing it is necessary for us to argue
in order to shape this poem in the flesh of a gentrified ear that has switched
from the bi-polarity of two governments, two opera orchestras in one city
I know you find great joy in the great but now you can put your lips to my understanding
in this room knowing the doors are locked and be faithful to the boredom
of a lesson that goes on this long and is only just halfway through
and yet it is alright, there is light and you are speaking too

EXHUMATION

I think you are good enough to not need me anymore
that is the responsibility of any speaker to recognise the coming of that moment
and accept it as a grenade that spins through the air towards us
what you will do with the knowledge is always interpretation though
it will always originate with me and the sources on the page I had the brilliance
to steal it from just this morning for this was won this morning unwashed
wet
perhaps it is a sign that aren't you glad there's still new lake like me in love with a person?
else what would thick city live on? they dig red noses blossomed with grappa
or so much beer it becomes a fest for the antiSchwabian
they dig the cold enough confusion to then push in your closed flat door
because of tissue in the cold being in the thousands today, for arriving
as a loosed door has new significance in this city so does the tunnel of hair
so does the scarf german pussy that wings more than two per bird
and winds around the strangle her with wool after I've finished reading
all the german girls need to do is go to sleep, quietly, when they don't awake again
all will be over with as far as my part is considered, having expressed what concerns
it's a shame john berryman killed himself unlike lesions lazarus
who are directly responsible for it becoming unaffordable in the face of like death
a force that cannot be interrupted or controlled as though it weren't somewhat
directly connected with decay and then death, the passing of generations
and their assorted fashions and trends that move the people like a pope to retire on a whim
to flush within and then without but I forget the city is twenty I'm reminded
and at twenty there were obvious futile that I too protested maybe wishing well
so an invasion of inhabitation mortality who couldn't get up afterward like a boxer
                    if she let me
then I know she's mental and should push back with my lips
play instrument to accompany my talking not singing in the hope the noise
is drowning a log in a waterpit in Egypt, the cemetery just up the road
in Prinzenallee surrounded by a fence that rises but inside is so profoundly quiet
that I watched the winter lotus grow from the crappy marble shining fingers
of the many German dead, or Turkish dead, as the time enough has passed
but it was in there, waiting for a shop to open, that I began and discovered
an exhumation of persuasiveness I really recommend you visit there I do

OBFUSCATION

Lesson five was not my finest lesson but I am not myself today
and yet this is the only day if you are following me properly
I can barely write down because my hands are so in and of my writing cold
which I alone to Alessandra owe and am waiting to have finished
though to force it finished is to know it shall not be so   which you understand
I pissed all over my hands to make them work again in Waldpflanzengarten
and a dog came to lick them clean   his spirituous beverages of impermanency (!)
impressed that he's not a bother to me two feet from my penis   exposed to the freezing cold
neologisms of the order of proximity ARE NECESSARY   canalou of a Clean
that is pure that is guilty
which is black tea with milk which happens like milk black of a certain time of day
but this is Balzac and the fat barista called Urban does not get the reference
parading a perfect coffee circle around a pile of dead bodies that had caught the plague
and now are being saturated with the incense from his censor and to think
he can carry on making young girls pregnant in a time of such disease
and that death doesn't put him off his strokes which repulse the soft stomached like I
who have much to listen to in Balzac but I keep walking
to find the paper tiger lotus peeler on sale
and once in Tangiers on a street as clean as this street a yellow dog bit me on the hand
it was the first time in my life and I decided that he was right
he was simply expressing in his own way that I was in the wrong
and I learned yet in southern Cyprus on a street cleaner than this street when a red dog
bit me on the hand and would not let go so he was not teaching me a lesson
so I placed the back of his skull to the headheight ruins of a concrete wall
from some forgotten insurrection nearby while he was still jawattached to my hand
and I used my free hand to slam my own bitten deep into the split of his jaw
ending the lesson there   audience applause

TREPANATION

those people going straight up to heaven where they have the time to write
a lot like us in this room but as residents you would have looked with eyes
walking from Prenzlauerberg to Neukolln and to see what I had seen = nothing much
only in Berlin could this be the case for accomplishment realising nothing of note
in a stretch of grey so long as to contain so many or something I understand the meaning
behind overheard conversation   pistorius / pastries
the back of a cricket bat spattered in blood
similar to a shop dedicated to poetry / dough   a writer, an artist, who really wants
to speak of / communicate that which is theirs that thing that is made up
of the many millions of ever multiplying experiences, that each are sense / affect and that
accumulate, as food in a stomach, that is the being of a schoolteacher whose students don't
speak a language, struck dumb simply do his best in failure of their future
where Wedding is cheap, and it's hard to make a living from ending it
though there is the dowry evaluated as a destination of human reception
each as a therapy for a learned body of men of women called a universitat
if I move here perhaps I'll wait, and friends will come to me like money in Sapped malls
I hear there they eat your guts as if I had the strength I might join in
picking up and making upon the stones   the darling little   the shopping
as some attempt to resist the shield grab of your sap and throw me tips
my scales ready to shield your   self in red flames   all your heaters bursting underground
to gas a load of Chinese former farmers   you have those right?   and your heaters too
to yours then   cheers   and I swoon heaters
and they're going their thing and changed from suns
which are really not toured me around to the old dragons who roam me   too stupid to lie
as if flowers in Templehof   Aeroflot dandelions having swords
ready to yourself from our catastrophic   argument that in turn shields eaters
        so get shields yourself from food that is bad for you
that is everywhere inside the gilded   the fish-bowled me   and aquariums drink your sap
and I like floating here nice and affordable   the window looks out on the hung seaweed
around my lips and I do at the glass night of the tar eaters with their hordes to tap

INHABITATION

tired these friends here are our last lesson poem, though I know to many of you
this will have been too long but it is nearly over so you can relax
walking home from an assuring I am climbing your city
consider me soon gone I have been given the opportunity to live in my wife's house
and act as a certain person who deserves money for being creatively busy
I will help his daughters as I am now saying how I might save you cannibals
that no matter poetry will not depravity many in a Shop front be as always free   ish
as it begins   to won't a … this was a crumble of the spine
a martial for fire dousing with water
& I do not enjoy dancing   even in a cared for like a child apartment
no matter what itinerant labouring class or race has popularised it as an escape
from the pain and drudgery of an anti-culture where they may not enjoy
the excess of the access that marks my first world mural
– a bear with a crown in Prenzlauerberg
a strung up befurred trophy goat in Neukolln
a ghost with a stomach in its heart and a mouth in its chest somewhere in Mitte
again your mind back to fights with arts you survived
with love in your hands here group of people
probably very few that I didn't mention my low expectation earlier to insult you
and you wish to live alone as we have been practised to do so
open only to the through gate accord of a father with a dead bloody rabbit
in one hand and a wish to teach shooting also in that hand
and the other being a desire for it to be cooked and recognised
you and all the one who truly wants to kill you
out of malice and memorised love the balanced one argument I have made over the last
half of your hour I know and I see you doing well   better than I at the end now
invited to a great gallery in front of them dresses and bored mouths like yours
up as I am a formerly violent frightened with big ears treading clumsy on your fingers
standing still in place not once having looked up after beginning with good in circles
not intruding too much into the message I carried out about this single room
though she expected applause or thanks or cast to when you were arguing back
which you shouldn't have because you might not even move to Berlin yet anyhow

wolves in chernobyl

today is nothing. the future won't come
Vasyl Stus

April 26th 1986

Ø

but even apart from our wood
I do not know how one should say
things in the dark have colour

will the wise do things,
things that are forbidden,
knowing it won't be found out?
a simple answer isn't easy to find
but freedom from trouble in the thing
and from pain in the thing
are still in the pleasure,
but joy in the thing, and exultation,
are considered, involving motion.

∅

all the day
life in the town goes on as normal
families shop and walk their dogs
fisherman lug their tackle off to the Prypyat river
couples sunbath around the cooling ponds
football matches go ahead
as do sixteen outdoor weddings
sponsored by the communist youth league

∅

how can an object be good if it withdraws the pleasures of taste,
(retreat for the cowardly)
and withdraws the pleasures of love…
and withdraws the pleasures of hearing…
the call of the button
and withdraws the pleasurable emotions caused to sight *by* beautiful
form?
yet it can be, good,
giving, living in the goodness of our wood.
by stable condition, by well-being,
by the sure hope of its continuance,
Kyiv, it was good, rightly calculated
do not eat green vegetables
or milk.

∅

the nature of the universe is things and void.
the nature of all existing things is body and space.
the nature of all space is things and colour.
if you wish to make me wealthy,
wish me not to make me glow,
but diminish my desire.

yet do not extinguish my desire,
allow me just enough left that I may not preach of being one,
or without desire, and above my peers,
but happy in the clutching of a ball
or an artist's postcard.
or a parents plot of land.
I hold in my hand my most precious object
– one's own pickled, cancerous appendix.

∅

I am thrilled with pleasure in the thing's body.
I spit black spit
on clear glass that is not somehow opaque
- or how we say 'frosted' – not for its own sake,
ancient armour, a gift from the basalt,
that blocks waves
because of the inconveniences that follow them.
With protection we may have a feast.

the schools debated whether or not to go ahead
with a planned 'Health run'
and settled on outdoor gymnastics instead

Ø

this is not anxious to please the mob.
for what pleases them, it does not know,
and what it does know is far removed from their comprehension.
it knows that when flesh cries aloud,
not possessing flesh,
it is unnatural that the mind should cry aloud too.
a silent stomach communicates in sweeping thoughts

Ø

it is better to be a thing of wool
and rag
that provokes freedom from fear
than a golden couch that brings trouble and woe.

sweet is the simple memory of a dead thing,
a friend,
a flag
and how one would not mind so much the joining of you both.

more firemen came up
complaining of vomiting and acute headaches

∅

if this wooden thing listened
to the prayers of all men,
all men would quickly have perished;
for they are forever praying death
against one another.

if the prayers of women were to come true…
of this i cannot speak, knowing not.

a foal had been born with eight legs
piglets without eyes
calves without heads or ribs.
        deformities due to inbreeding

∅

vain is the thing that does not heal suffering in man
for there is nothing new happening in the universe,
the warp closes like a mouth,
always readied for opening.

If we consider the infinite time passed,
and thus there is no excuse for distractions.
dumb things are for drowning,
thus the sea is deep.

helped us understand we are a colony

the newquay
as an english juarez poem

hot sun
i walk into a whorehouse

... then

o flying leukaemia
in your cloak like a living umbrella
a membrane of black leather which you unwind from within
yourself
lifted from the neck
flawless and bland

*

the rose of
lights
valley

*

and on all the roads to Moscow
the Flowers have grown legs to see the emperor

*

You love me I believe
when you believe I'm going to leave
which is often
I'm on the road 240 days a year
the first European in the West
the loose horses
became wild herds
more ordinary than before

*

I don't care what you're talking about
I want your children
we did a lot of shooting in Newquay
& a lot of surfing

Leaves

were it not for the spines
would it rather not be a fish backwards?
is it remarkable how much pain the bodies can endure?
the spiny po
      cket puffer grenade
the oligarch, raping his maid
spread, like the kit they call a test
that happens afterwards a fall
tap the hole right into the humunc
with a tap, or knife, or screw
whether it would then pour or been boiled
the men thereon were making most of Water
& stuck when a hole in them
like a tree syrup did leak out & they died
to comparison a human hand laid out all flat
would rather be gone at the start
of Alien on the eve of Prometheus
I am joy regretti
    ng

an easy way to loose a leaf
to drag bird shaped rocks from coal, as a cloud
& assuming, nothing will now abstain from grief
& mischief filth
a lost dog still must 'strain its greens'
as fingers that remain attached
were not meant to remain
                    clean
moving in, as a profession like marching
& now not to bring sheets
but plenty for the stuffing
the greened
unbroken
& brown flitter, the dropped
            Water
a mattress made of what is dead
& wonder, as are you a eunuch, of sorts
when they took your Cushion did they remove the pillow cases too?
if one only leaves were dry
girls
would we do
better?
to gyms, to learn how to fall?
rather to promote & produce
veins
thick & furious as intestinal
            parasites
to be a leafed, with rib
                    bons
run like android wires
    from our temple to our dick
there's a discussion for each
wed – & then retire, or work model

or rolling, or being first
& for each so many thousand, supporting others
each individual & courting such as the tree dies
& stupid it seemed in retrospect
big guns, fancy
are you scared at this part? you want to get out of here?
to a restaurant that serves Your food
the vestigial limb of your home
the Ent forest that is the real
made of marble
& horse,
the soup comes first
the bright start for the chlorophyll
while I have invested my money with zeal
into farms
built upon
orchards, who were family Oranges
now we get our fruit from the mare
        or from beneath ground
swine potato is our new apple
as Leaves are the gamblers
new tinted blue visor
we are lucky well fed
second son of the Family branch born a midget
        & looking back over the family tree
we see his wife was Dora Suarez
dead by axe
by cherry pluck, the red leaf like a land Owning lord
commanding an army of Midoclorian
because they are the things like make Leaf light
they fuel the plastic tunnel that blows us home
two golden stags fighting   overleaf
        or something of shape

just a hotter number – Food
when the heads are removed
these stags can be used as hollow cups
like the skinning of a bude
it breaks hexagonal like Buddha Tetris
& way the female bust is always probably Italian
her eyes and lips are Chinese
way the leaf covering her genitals
needs to be periodically changed
  & so love celebrated was back
home at work within my week & cavings
    we stuck to them windows
like a train journey interrupted bv falling debris
that has formed an incomparable couch inside eternity
    rice wrapped in heart on Dungeness
where art collective house purchases
     papered on the many are succulent fat Leaves
carrying the grape cross crucified Bride, shaking in wind
to symbolise the forgotten old gods of the north
           the Freya of the plant
a couchant hind as a pedant eating nothing but the finest
    forest like a mermaid
my friend of dappled light
of sea shade, I am a dragon
a milkmaid virgil
the lamb around here for grass shapes
I was sigil, shifting
but there are but two Strip
          clubs
& when returned from the Cave
we read the marriage book
& could not read it, the book of Leaves
for it read

'eid ma clack sharbo teppi ben ma'
now the black dolphin rises
with Leafs that look like Lions
& they are the libraries hibernating on their manes
as natural pillows
             translators
       who get paid nothing & who are not famous
in the kingdom of waving
                      funerals
out in the square
  one of my Brides had a broken nose
   as a dwarf animal pet had extended its paws
   then vinegar, like blood
was beetroot everywhere
The all is happening now as order
a way out through
             down
             obesity
so tuned in an animal course there was nothing left for us
  to eat
  you heard bears   & liked them with their garlands
        made up
an Emperor, ruling his peebles
knowing we need trees to breath
          protecting them with the dothraki host
which has no word for thankyou
       & I shouldn't have spoken to you like that
         while the Red leaves
who front the public room were dining places
     were anger all over our bruises
   my hurt mouth watching talk
  where I bashed you & buried you in season bulbs
the eco move is optimistic as the meat industrial complex

sells fat exclusively like lounges
> The space machine
> which is horse people

cutting the throats of their own horses
I've got such an anger problem
 it is a daily str
> uggle

that god blesses them
fuck drogue

the invasions of Britain
really began a culture of invasions
which had ramifications

*

and so the ghosts in their houses
of world politics
waiting for their chicken to cook

*

in the bed of the river so full of fish
hard to control the sense of it
upper lips accidentally causing offence

*

my enemy is my love
that has nothing to do with Mexico
rat heat and wealth

*

it is time to put the soft
toys aside
and begin the visual trick of walking downstairs

where there are no stairs
for this is rehearsal
for the grave

*

it is acceptable to stare at women on the congested train
and to flirt with with Lila
just fourteen years of visit

*

bitter to hit the farewell
the beach stretching into a red ocean
the sand littered with bardwire and death

Silk

{for thomas duggan}

<u>I.</u>

it is those who once flirted
with being overweight
          that loathe the fat.
THE FAT AS IN THE THING,
the white bags of it
not so much the people
      – bearing in mind
my friend has gone
        to be a fine novelist
included certainly in the best 30 under 30
while I am the struggling

with my first
novel

II.

honoured by the tongue
of a cow's skull
rotting teeth
in love
I pull you
down;
to the floor
of a wholesale silk supermarket run by a Han foreman
we must
whisper
our derision

III.

in chrysalis, do they roll ears?
what is safety
to their vehicle?
        do their convoys
need dickers?
to be allowed to touch tongue tone
with a beautiful latter day teen
silk espadrille
  hairless worm
    crimes
I hope, one day
to visit Tokyo

VI.

dye doping the silk with organique
ulling the nucleotides
that create DNA
to turn & ask
how do you cope with your past?
  have it computer modelled
into an Island, which disappears...
made one up from silk... containing rare seeds
which are protected
& then planted on time
in a future
(as the silk is to biodegrade)

V.

harvesting silk to sell at an uncompetitive
market, to rate
interest
but cultivation of worms is not free
& they are not growing towards light
the dry carapace lean toward
a net made from worm husks
given to the Sung
who don't yet
realise how damp the misery
is splayed across palms
a single grunt body dragging itself free

meditations on Strong tea

{for val raworth & tom raworth}

my tea is
  admirably
  complex

will it run the risk
  of being misunderstood?

*

sarcastic Chinese
 asking
why ... milk?
  because of breasts
& because udders just hang there
              otherwise

*

        the irony being
    on a journey to Edinburgh
    tae visit nick-e melville
      idon actually
          like
        hot drinks

★

you are the Shining Star of Bear Island
where all the trees
        have been stripped away
      to make room
          for the plantation's
        wives

hello chicken
        come visit. I will give you
        corn
          & stroke your head
      your feathers will be my handle;
        your skull will be my cup

                    ★

o man, I have Mark next to me
he stinks
    & has aspergers
    I could really do with a cup
        of Strong tea

★

my pleasure
    is derived from taste
    & clarity
    of expression
    my beverage is a nobel prize
        in a world
where dinner is an argument
        about Demolition man

★

I am happy
because I have
you
in my life

★

India is happening
    to England
        in Kenya
    & the Olympics
    are a bid
        for black granules
like Icelandic beaches

jolly ranchers swinging from a tree branch
a poison tree frog abuses a golden gibbon
'there are dragons up there'
he says, from the jungle floor
'& come drink my blood
it is ever so tasty'

★

I think that
Chinese River Dolphin
is a great name
for tea

★

I just want to dance with somebody
... with some
body who loves me ...
have you heard from ghost?
forgive her, for she knows not
what she does

★

Jublee, special brand
limited stocks
only for the people who read

★

I have paper for wedding
    poems
    but where will we hold
    the reception?
    in the dark star
  with the sugar compendium
                to bring up one that can drink up

        ★

fluffy bubble flying
    with a green parachute
  turns out to be a
      cancer tumour
  predicted in the scalextric

    I am the zoo
  the venice is a tea canal in sewage
    the swan is chased by the silver gorilla
                scotch in the white
                there are babies
                    in the way

        ★

                the elephant poet chooses
                its own interviewer
                in its small ears african dialect

a grape filled barrel boat
it makes wine through the medium
of flamenco

floating tea trunk
firing grapes like a cannon
asking me to clarify my questions

★

the King isn't in his castles
& dweebs have taken over
hell is real
I'm a brew of the moonstar
time is slowing, just 30 seconds are enough to break you here

★

my telestich always
unfortunately
ends in
T, E & A
which is a mint green
cardigan
for my lost child

★

there is but one town
            called Cambridge
but two parties called communities
  I mean communist
  red val runs relocation   at the townhall
  while pass the tea comrade darling
      holds a crop & promises valhalla he is coming

    glow trial or no
ex-foreign legion fluent french speaker
  getting used to British   manners
 asks his attackers
  'why are you being
            so mean?'
  in between bayonet thrusts
    he is at work again   no thanks to the gov't

                    ★

tea rots the gut
 if it is you
  who happens to drink it ...
  coffee fights cancer
 which is funny
  because it is black like Granada

                            ★

                the desert requires help
                  to cross
                  though Arab boys have strong backs
                  one has to feed their blasted
                  tutor

the dancing bear
               teaches hibernation
               how useful
               on such a long journey

               ★

the liquid breakfeast is a protean milkshake
    & what must be one
to realise the horror of the ceiling above
                    now they have two cats to clean for the milk is spilled

★

it's ok to spend
your life working
in Exeter Odeon
or Littlewood's
tea rooms because
when you're dead
there is nothing
which is like
a green tea with lots of peace

today there are hands I love
  yesterday it was an ape
tomorrow it will be herbs
   on the moon
  what is a chimp without teeth?
  what is a socket
     without an arm?
  an English sans T
     that is me

3 days a week
marvelling at the Swedish still life
getting a bone for the goth
    girls
  with the lip rings
  & bear tattoos
  in tribal breaks
  on lower back
        upper arse
              upper thighs
  whispering ghost warmings!
    the thursday rainbow stinks of perfume
      by bloody careful
        tattoos bleed, profusely

                    ★

I bring you seaweed
      emotional
    and yet, you just want tea...
    this will not work out
    migrant labourers died for this day
          I am a cup, a hand, a liquid
        the first in order, the last to run
              my wire lined servants suit
              I am butler to fools

          ★

I do hope we end
  up
  in a war with China
because
      I love killing
    peasants

*

Gregor Mendel is tending to his biscuit garden in the Tyrol...
        how stupid of me to not have thought of that!
                    the hereditary of strong tea is digital

                    *

        the tastiest biscuit
        is a fascist biscuit...
          but do we really need biscuits?

    *

like names in novels
  that are only initials...
    S.J. is conciliatory around the poetry table
    but rest assured
  he is hungry to hurt you
                doubters will doubt
                that not even heat becalmed
                  to just look down

it is the Czech republic in a French maid's uniform
but we'll be okay
like a frog on the forest floor
seeking coal for its lamp
we'll find a fire
to heat this tea
while haters hate themselves tiny:
skin coloured breasts in freedom
are contrary to the biting horse
filled with hate

que bonitos ochos tienes

these poems in 1984, the year after i was born.

*

the most country for journalists
an enormous black shed
built with the congealed blood of boats
and the bones of a free femicide, goat bones
my friend

*

they're in our bedrooms, our kitchen, our businesses
we don't hold out much hope
our daughters are perfect, such powerful forces
now we have road into the peoples sleep
which has spilled from red windows
and into the street of thousands

★

you are my employee
i reserve the right to punish you
for your monoply of decision
i have a bird shaped osmosis
of chemical hierarchy

★

there is more avenues of justice
now the withdrawn levers are students
in the roses of grass

★

endless screaming decapitations
steel and glass sushi bar
where children die
drowning in a marsh of clean slates
the monstrosity of honduras
banal bridges of clean massages

★

a lie to talk of a demarcation
a fraction of the legal / illegal economy
and a lie that the money class are against
for where does the money rest?
my portland road, my london banker
here is the new brand
violence as friendly, as a soldier on the street

★

id rather have the table at my Enemy
then eyeing me across the room

★

i want to take my children to the sea
so don't underestimate the word style
is an estimable word, where i come from
it is too late for deals

Epithalamia

{for david kelly & tiphaine mancaux}

TWENTY NINE YEARS

> whatever these two do
> is interesting
> *Anselm Hollo*

twenty nine years
to the day
I've hung a painting
of a mirror
it is your wedding
in Hackney
it is my birthday
in Beijing (Bilbao)
roadwork; a map to a pond
two mandarin ducks
symbolise
a long one

THE BRAINS GREY

the brain's grey
is a lateral
church
not yet figured
when the first
schisms on:
but pairs of people
will still pair

YOU WHO KNOWS WHITE

> how love begins
> I know full well
> but how it ends
> I do not know
> *Anselm Hollo*

who knows how white
attracts
yet always to keep herself
within black's shade
a flustered flower / a horse's broken leg
the generation who'll benefit from the inevitable expansion
of Cake inside the Sun
& the distinctly Crusader influence in the attitude to travel
storming walls
a bistro full of smoke sobbing into a cigar I hope

the pattern of humility displayed in view
of all who are
making case for the job they're doing

TRING

let no one be deceived
thinking that what they await
will last longer
than what they have seen
we are aware
that the invincible power that has moved the world
is unrequited, not fulfilled
love
but there are everything to limits

TREASURE

the symptoms of dawn
are perfect for not feeling happy
your bones have been aching since the small hours
your arsehole burns
& thunder threatens a storm
after three months of drought
at least though
before the blocked facade of Hackney Town Hall
you won't get stabbed
remember: if it burns
it's a sure & welcome sign
you still have one

DUNGENESS

> Yes I have spoken so softly and smiled so much
> my face has fallen away
> *Anselm Hollo*

the dover coast in harmoney
with dungeness
with lack of sleep
its hard to understand a language of
rain / trees + dead people
one could almost say they don't speak
our body full of bird
about to off in not a single
direction

a long, strange, happy (wordless) day
hanging wet trees

PROJECTION ROOM

limping toward
the Kawabe park cat cemetery
the trees that fence in the graves are green
the bushes that sprout between the stones are blue
Mr.Sugiwara has a new personal assistant
Ms.Kelly-Mancaux
tenticles flapping

INJURY

> in love we loaf
> munching love's leaf
> it is a fortunate condition
> *Anselm Hollo*

I banged my head on the window
my skin on the table
I certainly did not cry mother god
or courage
but livia, to come & comfort me
for I was hurt

TURBULENCE

quite intense turbulence
scribbles my writing
drunk Rob staggers to his seat
red wine lips pulled back
in amazement
if we survive
I'll do little different

THE FANATICS

> There is pain,
> who can deny it
> *Anselm Hollo*

the fanatics are for the confines of a tearoom
in opposition to the vastness of the universe
are you prepared to die for an object?
well ... danny dyer returns to his manor

I am number 3
good to hear that is high on the charm scale

The Truth is that they are to blame for not concealing
and not concealing is a shameful thing
instead making an ostentatious show of love

INHERITANCE

> the dashing biologist
> "with the looks of a viking"
> *Anselm Hollo*

my only inheritance argument
between brothers
over swords
glyn has a son & wins
but I get Magnus Magnussen
& an axe
steward of the fat dog
glue of strategy misheard
Hnefatafl
in front room of Newquay
full of bright Fish

ON YOUR BIRTHDAY

> yes he wants a gun
> like everybody
> but at least he
> doesn't claim it's
> 'for protection'
> *Anselm Hollo*

on your birthday
I wrote you an entire
flipbook of poems
cruelty deafens me secret

strange lovely daughter I have banished
I recall some were of the tube
as a single flake
of another man's scalp
falls upon me now

THE MEANS OF REMEMBERING

> well everything's pretty great really
> but for poverty illness mortality and so on
> *Anselm Hollo*

the means of remembering the room
will always be a light up remembered
some measurable pace in moments
that are passing happening
guts to see patents dying
man to god is panelled by hardening
    it gets worse the longer it goes on
nearly twenty seven years in the whole
lions in the nursery, going plastic / never alive

ON THE LEDGE

on the ledge of electronic correspondence
with china / it is not a conversation
nature I thought I like you
did I miss out in my thanks
all these years I've not yet lived?
catherine has had a day off today
so I'll be alone
two are walking the green roof
these opportunities I cannot accept
for I married properly

ACKNOWLEDGED IN MULTITUDE

> the energy of the world has grown
> tired
> of our green &
> bumbling
> *Anselm Hollo*

we acknowledge dearth in multitude
as we acknowledge for humanity
we have failed apes / but for apes
we look this monkey strums a stringbox
& speaks over his own facticity with lyrics
which disrobe his emotional happenings
as though they were doctor's appointments
& do no more
no acoustic weddings are fair, its invitations

DEAD SOULS

> watching the spectacle of the money
> come to an end
> things become clear
> *Anselm Hollo*

Gogol burns his manuscript for fear
that they would escape into the earth
& be for moles to laugh about at
& here's blowing dust from a petrified
its a scam migration begins
the pentagon disintegrates & I'm happy it
thanks bit I'm a emotional epic
delighted you're escaping for a purpose
into another

RING FINGER

> but really my parents
> you were giant white rabbit people
> *Anselm Hollo*

I attempt to bore a sized finger hole
into the random embarrassing use
of what expression does the human face
take when the head has lost it's bodY?
these are the questions we must consider
a crack in the road that might be worth going
round reason yesterday I had a sudden fear

that you were in trouble / the opposite encased
as whatever doesn't let you / gets you later

THE WELL

> I enjoy saying it
> so slowly
> *Anselm Hollo*

wanted as the mother of a sun who would revenge me
a number by its very presence

a cheeseboard shaped like a cow
a hand sized staple over a special book
a full mouse disguised as just the head of an axlotl
I never thought I'd get this lonely
of these many evenings passed this one, spent writing
is a monad, an orb, a friend
but as long as you're trying to change
its not as though I lived through what they lived through
& so was able
to write what they wrote anyway

INSECTS

at times it seems merely a question of how to abdicate
Anselm Hollo

the
insects roof dried
the chinese countryside would hold us for property / spirits
of unimaginable affordability;
credit to our time together
eternally too brief
that a mirroring to have been a new kind between four
corners as evidence
squarefalling double in greenland
terrible trouble without you
but you will be fine
we can all crow
that it'd be
better if no one
every did / marry but
we are you to love
that's a good end

ENDNOTES

'Atacama' was previously published by *Dusie*, and featured in the 2013 Ars Poetica festival anthology, translated into Slovakian.

'Atacama', 'Calling the doctor makes me feel better', 'They let me have his books', 'The Newquai as an English Juarez poem', 'That god blesses them fuck drogue' and 'Que bonitos ochos tienes' were written for the Enemigos project, a transliterative exchange between poets from London and Mexico City. They previously appeared in the Enemigos anthology, translated into Spanish.

'Wormwood Scrubs' was previously published by *Exquisite Corpse*.

'the Rasenna' was written for a collaboration with the artist David Kelly, and was exhibited in the My Pixxa gallery, Farringdon, London in 2012. A selection was published by *Rattle* magazine.

'Scent' was commissioned by Lush, for the Golden hour tour, in 2012. A selection was published by *Recours au Poeme*, translated into French.

'Wildermenn' was written for a collaboration with the artists David Kelly, Ben Morris and Robert Hitzeman, and was exhibited at the House Gallery, Peckham, London, in 2013.

'Wortwedding' was written for a collaboration with the artist Alessandra Eramo, and was exhibited in the Wortwedding gallery, Wedding, Berlin in 2013. A selection was published by *Zone* magazine.

'Wolves in Chernobyl' was previously published by *Counterexample poetics*.

'Leaves' was commissioned by Very Small Kitchen and published previously as an ebook.

'Silk' was written for a collaboration with the artist Thomas Duggan, and after being printed in synthetic silk, was exhibited in the Hardy Tree gallery, Kings Cross, London in 2013. The poems also appeared in full in the *Wolf* magazine.

'meditations on Strong tea' was commissioned by Zimzalla and the Poetea project, and published previously as an ebook.

EYEWEAR PUBLISHING